KNOCK KNOCK JOKES FOR KIDS

A JOKE BOOK FOR CHILDREN

M. PREFONTAINE

Published by MP Publishing

Knock, knock.
  Who's there?
Lettuce.
  Lettuce who?
Lettuce in, it's cold out here.

Knock, knock.
  Who's there?
Wooden shoe.
  Wooden shoe who?
Wooden shoe like to hear another joke?

Knock, knock.
  Who's there?
Watson.
  Watson who?
What's on TV tonight?

Knock, knock.
  Who's there?
Atch.
  Atch who?
Bless you!

Knock, knock.
  Who's there?
A broken pencil.
  A broken pencil who?
Oh never mind it's pointless.

Knock, knock.
  Who's there?
Boo!
  Boo who?
Don't cry, it's just me.

Knock, Knock.
   Who's there?
Who.
   Who who?
Are you an owl?

Knock, Knock!
   Who's there?
Abby.
   Abby who?
Abby birthday to you

Knock, Knock.
   Who's there?
Cash.
   Cash who?
I knew you were a nut!

Knock, knock.
  Who's there?
Tank.
  Tank who?
Your welcome.

Knock, knock!
  Who's there?
Annie.
  Annie who?
Annie body home?

Knock, knock.
  Who's there?
Cook.
  Cook who?
Hey! Who are you calling cuckoo?

Knock, knock.
 Who's there?
Harry.
 Harry who?
Harry up, it's cold out here.

Knock, knock.
 Who's there?
Spell.
 Spell who?
W-H-O.

Knock, Knock.
 Who's there?
Rover.
 Rover who?
Rover the hill.

Knock, knock.

Who's there?

Norma Lee.

Norma Lee who?

Norma Lee I don't go around knocking on doors, but I just had to meet you.

Knock, knock

Who's there?

Iva.

Iva who?

I've a sore hand from knocking.

Knock, knock.

Who's there?

Avenue.

Avenue who?

Avenue knocked on this door before?

Knock, knock.
  Who's there?
Noah.
  Noah who?
Noah good place we can get something to eat?

Knock, knock.
  Who's there?
Ice cream.
  Ice cream who?
Ice cream if you don't let me in.

Knock, knock.
  Who's there?
A titch.
  A titch who?
Bless you.

Knock, knock.
  Who's there?
Turnip.
  Turnip who?
Turnip the volume, it's quiet in here.

Knock, knock.
  Who's there?
Goat.
  Goat who?
Goat to the door and find out.

Knock, knock.
  Who's there?
Howard.
  Howard who?
Howard I know?

Knock, knock.
 Who's there?
Nobel.
 Nobel who?
No bell, that's why I knocked.

Knock, knock.
 Who's there?
Me.
 Me who?
Wow! You don't know who you are?

Knock, knock.
 Who's there?
Hawaii.
 Hawaii who?
I'm fine. Hawaii you.

Knock, knock.

Who's There?

Theodore.

Theodore who?

Theodore is stuck and it won't open.

Knock, Knock.

Who's there?

Russell.

Russell who?

Russell up something to eat.

Knock, Knock.

Who's there?

Dozen.

Dozen who?

Dozen anybody want to let me in?

Knock, Knock.
Who's there?
Doughnut.
Doughnut Who?
Doughnut ask, it's a secret.

Knock, Knock.
Who's there?
Ya.
Ya Who?
What are you so excited about?

Knock, Knock.
Who's there?
I am.
I am who?
You don't know who you are?

Knock, knock.
  Who's there?
Amos.
  Amos who?
A mosquito.

Knock, knock.
  Who's there?
Anudder
  Anudder who?
Anudder mosquito.

Knock, Knock.
  Who's there?
Abbott.
  Abbott who?
Abbott time you opened this door.

Knock, Knock.

Who's there.

Tuna?

Tuna who?

You can tuna a piano, but you can't tuna fish.

Knock, Knock.

Who's there?

Vlad.

Vlad who?

Vlad to meet you.

Knock, Knock

Who's there.

Greece.

Greece who.

Greece my palm and I'll tell you.

Knock, Knock.
  Who's there?
Voodoo.
  Voodoo who?
Voodoo you think you are?

Knock, Knock.
  Who's there?
Heaven.
  Heaven who?
Heaven seen you for a long time.

Knock, Knock.
  Who's there ?
Kenya.
  Kenya who?
Kenya guess who is it?

Knock, Knock.
  Who's there?
Russian.
  Russian who?
Russian about makes me tired.

Knock, Knock.
  Who's there?
Miles.
  Miles who?
Miles away.

Knock, Knock.
  Who's there?
Modem.
  Modem who?
Modem lawns, grass is getting high.

Knock, Knock.

Who's there?

Nana.

Nana who?

Nana your business.

Knock, Knock.

Who's there?

Philip.

Philip who?

Philip my glass will you please.

Knock, Knock.

Who's there?

Pudding.

Pudding who?

Pudding on your shoes before your trousers is a bad idea.

Knock, Knock.

Who's there?

Rain.

Rain who?

Rain dear, you know, Rudolph the red nosed rain dear.

Knock, Knock.

Who's there?

Safari.

Safari who?

Safari so good.

Knock, Knock.

Who's there?

Sharon.

Sharon who?

Sharon share alike.

Knock, Knock.

Who's there?

Sid.

Sid who?

Sid down and have a cup of tea.

Knock, Knock.

Who's there?

Sinker.

Sinker who?

Sinker swim, it's up to you.

Knock, Knock.

Who's there?

Thermos.

Thermos who?

Thermos be a better knock knock joke than this.

Knock, Knock.
  Who's there?
Thistle.
  Thistle who?
Thistle be the last time I knock on this door.

Knock, Knock.
  Who's there?
Carrie.
  Carrie who?
Carrie me home, I'm tired.

Knock, Knock
  Who's there?
Cliff.
  Cliff who?
Cliff hanger.

Knock, Knock.

Who's there?

Cook.

Cook who?

Cuckoo yourself, I don't come here to be insulted.

Knock, Knock.

Who's there?

Snow.

Snow who?

Snow use, I've forgotten my key again.

Knock, Knock.

Who's there?

Spider .

Spider who?

I spider with my little eye.

Knock, Knock
Who's there?
Stan.
Stan who?
Stan back, I'm knocking the door down.

Knock, Knock.
Who's there?
Tuba.
Tuba who?
Tuba toothpaste.

Knock, Knock.
Who's there?
Twig.
Twig who?
Twig or tweat.

Knock, Knock.
 Who's there?
Witches.
 Witches who?
Witches the way to go home.

Knock, Knock.
 Who's there?
Yee.
 Yee who?
What? Are you a cowboy?

Knock, Knock.
 Who's there?
Yukon.
 Yukon who?
Yukon lead a horse to water, but you can't make it drink.

Knock, Knock.

Who's there ?

Zoom.

Zoom who?

Zoom did you expect.

Knock, knock.

Who's there?

Water.

Water who?

Water way to answer the door.

Knock, Knock.

Who's there?

Broccoli.

Broccoli who?

Broccoli doesn't have a last name, silly.

Knock, Knock.
  Who's there?
Justin.
  Justin who?
Justin time for lunch.

Knock, knock.
  Who's there?
Alex.
  Alex who?
Alex-plain later.

Knock, knock.
  Who's there?
CD.
  CD who?
CD guy on your doorstep?

Knock, Knock.
  Who's there?
Denise.
  Denise who?
Denise are above your ankles.

Knock, knock.
  Who's there?
Merry.
  Merry who?
Merry Christmas.

Knock, Knock.
  Who's there?
Sacha.
  Sacha who?
Sacha lot of questions.

Knock, Knock.
Who's there?
Des.
Des who?
Des no bell, dat's why I'm knocking.

Knock, knock.
Who's there?
Noah.
Noah who?
Noah good place we can get something to eat?

Knock, Knock.
Who's there?
Diesel.
Diesel who?
Diesel make you feel better.

Knock, Knock.

Who's there?

Sam.

Sam who?

Sam person who knocked on the door last time.

Knock, Knock.

Who's there?

Dishes.

Dishes who?

Dishes a very bad joke.

Knock, knock.

Who's there?

Alpaca.

Alpaca who?

Alpaca the trunk, you pack the suitcase.

Knock, Knock.

Who's there?

Dismay.

Dismay who?

Dismay be a joke but it doesn't make me laugh.

Knock, knock.

Who's there?

Scot.

Scot who?

Scot nothing to do with you.

Knock, Knock.

Who's there?

Doctor.

Doctor who?

That's right - where's my tardis?

Knock, Knock.
   Who's there?
Sandy.
   Sandy who?
Sandy door, I just got a splinter.

Knock, Knock.
   Who's there?
Duck.
   Duck who?
Just duck. They're throwing things at us.

Knock, Knock.
   Who's there?
Scissor.
   Scissor who?
Scissor and Cleopatra.

Knock, knock.

Who's there?

Isabel.

Isabel who?

Isabel working? I had to knock.

Knock, Knock.

Who's there?

Alec.

Alec who?

Alec-tricity. Isn't that a shock?

Knock, Knock.

Who's there?

Duke.

Duke who?

Duke come here often.

Knock, Knock.
   Who's there?
Alec.
   Alec who?
Alec my lolly.

Knock, Knock.
   Who's there?
Dwayne.
   Dwayne who?
Dwayne in Spain falls mainly on the plain...

Knock, Knock.
   Who's there?
Alison.
   Alison who.
Alison Wonderland.

Knock, Knock.
   Who's there?
Dwight.
   Dwight who?
Dwight way and the wrong way.

Knock, Knock.
   Who's there?
Alma.
   Alma who?
Alma not going to tell you.

Knock, Knock.
   Who's there?
Dan.
   Dan who?
Dan Druff.

Knock, Knock.
Who's there?
Alpaca.
Alpaca who?
Alpaca picnic lunch.

Knock, Knock.
Who's there?
Dana.
Dana who?
Dana talk with your mouth full.

Knock, Knock.
Who's there?
Amahl.
Amahl who?
Amahl shook up.

Knock, Knock.
  Who's there?
Datsun.
  Datsun who?
Datsun old joke.

Knock, Knock.
  Who's there?
Ammonia.
  Ammonia who?
Ammonia little boy who can't reach the doorbell.

Knock, Knock.
  Who's there?
Della.
  Della who?
Della-katessen.

Knock, Knock.
Who's there?
Annie.
Annie who?
Annie-versary.

Knock, Knock.
Who's there?
Attila.
Attila who?
Attila you no lies.

Knock, Knock
Who's there?
Augusta.
Augusta who?
Augusta wind will blow the witch away.

Knock, Knock.
Who's there?
Auntie.
Auntie who?
Auntie glad to see me again.

Knock, Knock.
Who's there?
Ear.
Ear who?
Ear you are, I've been looking for you.

Knock, Knock.
Who's there?
Bee.
Bee who?
Bee careful.

Knock, Knock.
  Who's there?
Frank.
  Frank who?
Frankenstien.

Knock, Knock.
  Who's there?
Ears.
  Ears who?
Ears looking at you.

Knock, Knock.
  Who's there?
Bacon.
  Bacon who?
Bacon a cake for your birthday.

Knock, Knock.
  Who's there?
Ellie.
  Ellie who?
Ellie Phants never forget.

Knock, Knock.
  Who's there?
Boo.
  Boo who?
Just Boo. I'm a ghost.

Knock, Knock.
  Who's there?
Bet.
  Bet who?
Bet you don't know who's knocking on your door.

Knock, Knock
　　Who's there?
Barbie.
　　Barbie who?
Barbie Q.

Knock, Knock.
　　Who's there?
Flea.
　　Flea who?
Flea's a jolly good fellow.

Knock, Knock.
　　Who's there?
Furry.
　　Furry who?
Furry's a jolly good fellow.

Knock, Knock.
Who's there?
Four Eggs.
Four Eggs who?
Four Eggs ample.

Knock, Knock.
Who's there?
Francis.
Francis who?
Francis next to Germany.

Knock, Knock.
Who's there?
Ho-ho.
Ho-ho who?
You know, your Santa impression could use a little work.

Knock, Knock
  Who's there?
Chile.
  Chile who?
Chile out tonight.

Knock, Knock.
  Who's there?
Chair.
  Chair who?
Chair you go again, asking more questions.

Knock, Knock.
  Who's there?
Mary and Abbey.
  Mary and Abbey who?
Mary Christmas and Abbey New Year.

Knock, Knock

Who's there?

Chest.

Chest who?

Chest-nuts for sale.

Knock, Knock.

Who's there?

Snow.

Snow who?

Snow use. I forgot my name again.

Knock, Knock.

Who's there?

Catsup.

Catsup who?

Catsup on the roof.

Knock, Knock
  Who's there?
Colleen.
  Colleen who?
Colleen up your room, it's filthy.

Knock, Knock.
  Who's there?
Gus.
  Gus who?
That's what you're supposed to do.

Knock, Knock.
  Who's there?
Hal.
  Hal who?
Hallo to you too.

Knock, knock.
   Who's there?
Cows go.
   Cows go who?
No you idiot, cows go mooo.

Knock, Knock.
   Who's there?
Gary.
   Gary who?
Gary on smiling.

Knock, knock.
   Who's there?
Kanga.
   Kanga who?
Actually, it's kangaroo.

Knock, knock.
  Who's there?
Beats.
  Beats who?
Beats me.

Knock, Knock
  Who's there?
Hardy.
  Hardy who?
Hardy recognized you.

Knock, knock.
  Who's there?
An extraterrestrial.
  Extraterrestrial who?
What – how many extra-terrestrials do you know?

Knock, Knock
Who's there?
Genoa.
Genoa who?
Genoa any new jokes?

Knock, knock.
Who's there?
Justin.
Justin who?
Justin the neighborhood, mind if I come in for a chat?

Knock, knock.
Who's there?
Dozen.
Dozen who?
Dozen all this knocking bother you already?

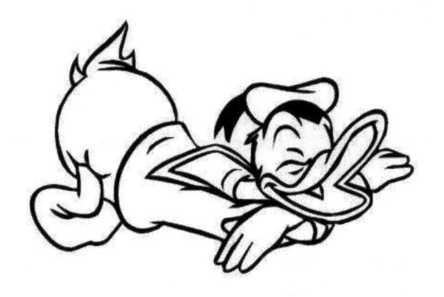

Knock, Knock
Who's there?
Gladys.
Gladys who?
Gladys Friday, aren't you.

Knock, knock.
Who's there?
Snow.
Snow who?
Snow point pretending you don't know me.

Knock, Knock.
Who's there?
Grant.
Grant who?
Grant you a wish, what is it?

Knock, Knock
  Who's there?
Haifa.
  Haifa who?
Haifa cake is better than none.

Knock, Knock.
  Who's there?
Hey.
  Hey who?
Hey ho, hey ho, it's off to work we go.

Knock, Knock.
  Who's there?
Kermit.
  Kermit who?
Kermit a crime and you'll get locked up.

Knock, Knock
Who's there?
Jess.
Jess who?
I give up, who?

Knock, Knock.
Who's there?
Knee.
Knee who?
Knee-d you ask.

Knock, Knock.
Who's there?
Juicy.
Juicy who?
Juicy what I just saw.

Knock, Knock.
Who's there?
Lady.
Lady who ?
Lady law down.

Knock, Knock
Who's there?
Jean.
Jean who?
Jeanius - you just don't recognise it.

Knock, Knock.
Who's there?
Larva.
Larva who?
Larva cup of coffee.

Knock, Knock.
Who's there?
Jester.
Jester who?
Jester minute I'm trying to find my keys.

Knock, Knock.
Who's there?
Lass.
Lass who?
That's what cowboys use, isn't it?

Knock, Knock.
Who's there?
James.
James who?
James people play.

Knock, Knock.

Who's there?

Laurie.

Laurie who?

Laurie load of goodies.

Knock, Knock.

Who's there?

I don't know.

I don't know who?

I told you I don't know. Why don't you believe me?

Knock, Knock.

Who's there?

Luke.

Luke who?

Luke and see who it is.

Knock, Knock.
  Who's there?
Hip.
  Hip who?
Hippopotamus.

Knock, Knock.
  Who's there?
Mabel.
  Mabel who?
Mabel syrup is lovely on puddings.

Knock, Knock.
  Who's there?
Jerry.
  Jerry who?
Jerry funny, let me in.

Knock, Knock.
  Who's there?
Mae.
  Mae who?
Mae be I'll tell you or Mae be I won't.

Knock, Knock.
  Who's there?
Jack.
  Jack who?
Jackpot.

Knock, Knock.
  Who's there?
Man.
  Man who?
Managed to get here then.

Knock, Knock.

Who's there?

Hole.

Hole who?

Hole-he cow Batman, to the Bat Mobile.

Knock, Knock.

Who's there?

Manchu.

Manchu who?

Manchu your food six times at least.

Knock, Knock.

Who's there?

Jeff.

Jeff who?

Jeff in one ear, shout.

Knock, Knock
   Who's there?
Jaws.
   Jaws who?
Jaws truly.

Knock, Knock
   Who's there?
Maxie.
   Maxie who?
Maxie-mum.

Knock, Knock.
   Who's there?
Manny.
   Manny who?
Manny people keep asking me that.

Knock, Knock.
   Who's there?
Jamaica.
   Jamaica who?
Jamaica mistake.

Knock, Knock.
   Who's there?
Howard.
   Howard who?
Howard can it be to guess a knock knock joke?

Knock, Knock
   Who's there?
Me.
   Me who?
I didn't know you had a cat.

Knock, Knock.
Who's there?
Kareem.
Kareem who?
Kareem of the crop.

Knock, Knock.
Who's there?
Mice.
Mice who?
Mice to meet you.

Knock, Knock
Who's there?
Hugh.
Hugh who?
Hugh's afraid of the big bad wolf!

Knock, Knock.
  Who's there?
Mike.
  Mike who?
Mike-robe.

Knock, Knock.
  Who's there?
Kay.
  Kay who?
Kay,L,M,N,O,P,Q,R,S,T,U,V,W,X,Y,Z.

Knock, Knock.
  Who's there?
Moose.
  Moose who?
Moose you be so nosy?

Knock, Knock.

Who's there?

Jess.

Jess who?

Jess me and my shadow.

Knock, Knock.

Who's there?

Norma.

Norma who?

Norma'lly I have my key.

Knock, Knock.

Who's there?

Plato.

Plato who?

Plato fish and chips please.

Knock, Knock.

Who's there?

Paine.

Paine who?

Paine in the neck.

Knock, knock.

Who's there?

Canoe.

Canoe who?

Canoe help me with my homework?

Knock, Knock.

Who's there?

Nose.

Nose who?

I nose plenty more knock knock jokes, don't worry.

Knock, knock.
Who's there?
Anee.
Anee,who?
Anee one you like.

Knock, Knock.
Who's there?
Pat.
Pat who?
Pat yourself on the back.

Knock, knock.
Who's there?
A herd.
A herd who?
A herd you were home, so I came over.

Knock, Knock.

Who's there?

Ocelot.

Ocelot who?

Ocelot of questions don't you.

Knock, knock.

Who's there?

Adore.

Adore who?

Adore is between us. Open up.

Knock, Knock.

Who's there?

Pear.

Pear who?

Pear of shoes.

Knock, knock
   Who's there?
Water
   Water who?
Water you doing in my house?

Knock, Knock.
   Who's there?
Oil.
   Oil who?
Oil be seeing you then.

Knock, Knock.
   Who's there?
Pecan.
   Pecan who?
Pecan work it out.

Knock, knock.

Who's there?

Beef.

Beef who?

Before I get cold, you'd better let me in.

Knock, Knock.

Who's there.

Olivia.

Olivia who?

Olivia but I lost the key.

Knock, knock.

Who's there?

Yukon.

Yukon who?

Yukon say that again.

Knock, Knock.
Who's there?
Ooze.
Ooze who?
Ooze been sleeping in my bed.

Knock, knock.
Who's there?
Amy.
Amy who?
Amy fraid I've forgotten.

Knock, Knock.
Who's there?
Pinza.
Pinza who?
Pinza needles.

Knock, knock.
  Who's there?
Amanda.
  Amanda who?
A man da fix your sink.

Knock, Knock.
  Who's there?
Pierre.
  Pierre who?
Pierre through the keyhole, you'll see.

Knock, Knock.
  Who's there?
Radio.
  Radio who?
Radi-o-not, here I come.

Knock, Knock.
  Who's there?
Orson.
  Orson who?
Orson cart.

Knock, Knock.
  Who's there?
Figs.
  Figs who?
Figs the doorbell, it's broken.

Knock, Knock.
  Who's there?
Pizza.
  Pizza who?
Pizza cake would be great right now.

Knock, Knock.

Who's there?

Oscar.

Oscar who?

Oscar a silly question, get a silly answer.

Manufactured by Amazon.ca
Bolton, ON

15714039R00044